I0423886

"Breaking News"

How and Why Donald Trump Will Win the 2016 Presidential Election

By David Coleman

"Breaking News"

How and Why Donald Trump will win the 2016
Presidential Election

By David Coleman

Donald Trump will be the next president of the United States. He will beat Hillary Clinton and end the Clintons political history. He will win because in America a white man will always win against a white woman for president. That is because most white men and many white women do not want to see a white woman in such a powerful position. White men would prefer a white woman stay home and bake the cookies, as Hillary Clinton once said she was not willing to do, even though they will not say it publically. Many women, white or black are always jealous of other successful women. That is why they will vote for Donald Trump even though they dislike him. The same was true in 2008 when Barack Obama defeated Hillary Clinton. Voters chose a black man over a white woman.

It requires 270 Electoral votes to become president of the United States. Each state has electoral votes based on their size and population. This election will be a landslide for "The Donald." Here is a state by state breakdown on how and why he will become the next President of the United States of America.

All voters should remember. It takes 270 electoral votes to become president. So if I was running for president and got 100,000.00 votes but my opponent got 80,000.00 he or she could still win depending on the electoral votes they have won. This year will be the most critical for the electoral vote, not the popular vote. So everyone should pay attention to the states that are won.

Alabama, 9 Electoral Votes

Donald Trump: Winner

Alabama. Alabama has 9 electoral votes. No democratic candidate has won this state in the last 20 years. In this year's Republican Primary Donald Trump got over 700,000 votes. The Democrats got only 400,000 votes. Alabama is the home of George Wallace, one of the most racist governors in the history of the United States. There are still many racist in the state and they will come out in droves to vote for Trump. They still believe that a woman place is in the home and not out working. This will not even be close. Trump will win this state by a landslide. Jimmy Carter was the last democratic presidential candidate to win the state. That was back in 1976.

Alaska, 3 Electoral Votes

Winner: Donald Trump

Alaska. Alaska has 3 electoral votes. The state has not voted for a democratic presidential candidate since 1976. That was when Republican Barry Goldwater lost to Lyndon Johnson. Donald Trump is divisive but not nearly as bad as Barry Goldwater. Its most famous Republican, Sarah Palin is from here. Donald will win this state easily.

Arizona, 11 Electoral Votes

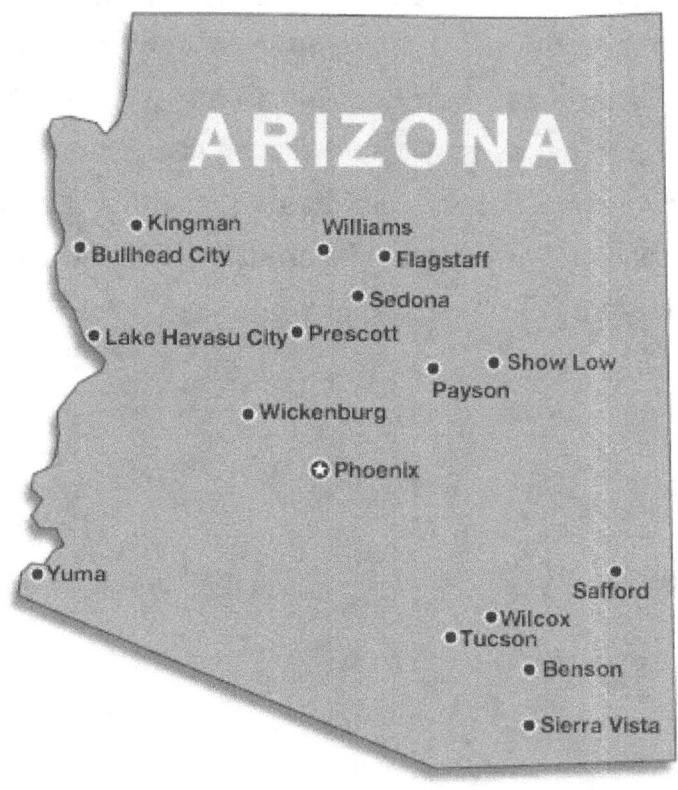

Donald Trump: Winner

Arizona. My oh my has Arizona grown. In 1960 Arizona had only 4 electoral votes. Today they have 11. It is one of the fastest growing states in the country. Of course a lot of it is because of Mexicans pouring in over the border and legal immigrants having babies. This is a republican state but will change to democrat in about 10 years. Bill Clinton is the only Democratic Presidential candidate to win the state the last 40 years. That was back in 1996. That should help Hillary put up a good fight here, but not enough to win. Trump wins Arizona.

Arkansas, 6 Electoral Votes

Donald Trump: Winner

Arkansas. Arkansas has 6 electoral votes. It is my home state. I grew up in Texarkana and studied at the University of Arkansas at Fayetteville. I am a Razorback through and through. The last time a democratic presidential candidate won here was Bill Clinton in 1996. So you would think that Hillary has a chance here, not. The state is like most other southern states when it comes to women. It is anti-abortion, against gay rights, against a higher minimum wage, and so forth. It definitely believes that a woman's place is home not running a country. I will never forget my friends telling me that that best place to keep a woman was barefoot and pregnant. That has not changed much. Donald Trump will take my home state easily.

California, 55 Electoral Votes

Winner: Hillary Clinton

California. California has 55 electoral votes. It has more electoral votes than any other state. It is set up perfectly for Hillary Clinton to win. White men do not dominate the scene. There are many Latinos, blacks, Asians, Muslims, and other ethnic groups. It has been over 25 years since Californians voted for a republican presidential candidate. You can add to those years. Hillary wins California.

Colorado, 9 Electoral Votes

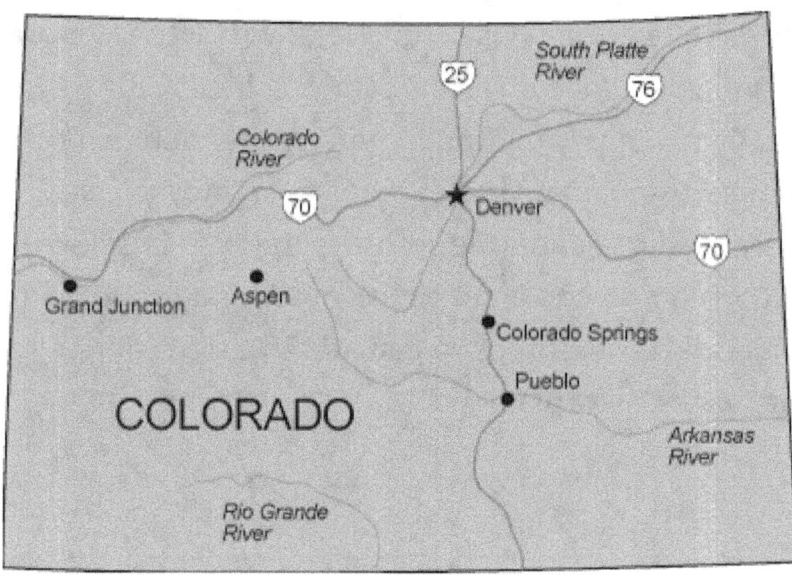

Hillary Clinton: Winner

Colorado. Colorado has 9 Electoral votes. Barak Obama won the state the last two presidential elections. For that reason I think that Hillary Clinton will win the state. But I am not 100% sure about this one. I already have Donald Trump winning this election by a landslide. Just think if he won Colorado he could end up to close to 400 electoral votes. Remember he only needs 270 to become president. This state is ready made for him. They have the most progressive marijuana laws in the country. That tells me that they are antiestablishment. It is a white state. 78% of the state is white, only 13% black. Remember a black man is more important than a white woman to many white men who vote, it made it easier to vote for Barack Obama than to vote for Hillary Clinton. There are no blacks and Latinos to help her out here. Trump should be able to get those votes. Hillary also lost earlier this year to Bernie Sanders here in the primary. Today is May 5, 2016. If I were Donald Trump I would set up a big office in Colorado. I am giving this state to Hillary, but it is begging for Trump.

Connecticut, 7 Electoral Votes

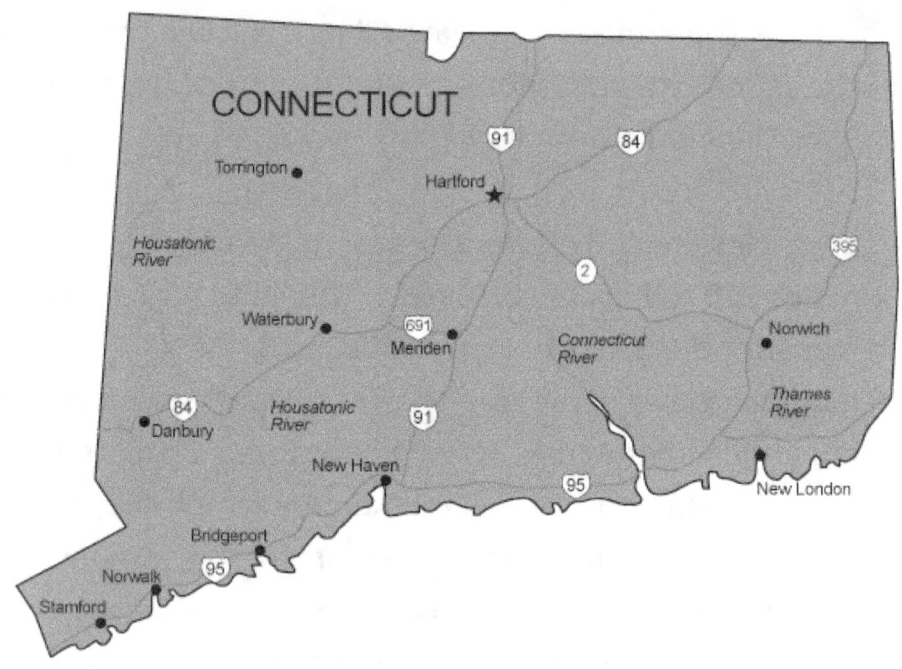

Winner: Hillary Clinton

Connecticut. Connecticut has 7 electoral votes. It has voted for the Democratic Presidential candidate the last 6 elections. I see no reason for it to change this time. Hillary will win this state easily. It is also next to her home state of New York.

Delaware, 3 Electoral Votes

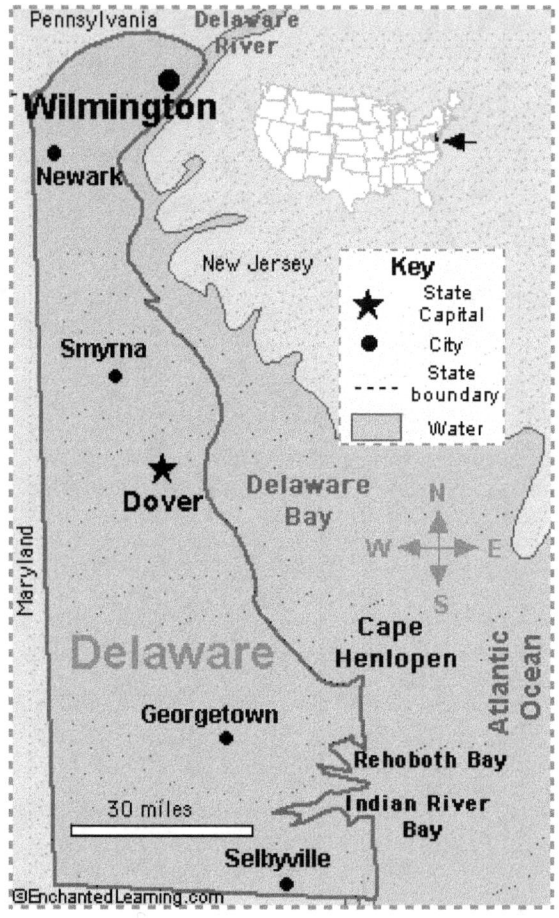

Hillary Clinton: Winner

Delaware. Delaware has 3 electoral votes. It has not voted for a republican presidential candidate since 1988. It will not in 2016 either. Hillary Clinton will win easily. Vice president Joe Biden is from the state also.

Florida, 29 Electoral Votes

Winner: Donald Trump

Florida. Florida, Florida, Florida. Florida has 29 electoral votes and is always in the forefront in determining our next president. It was the state that ended the political career of All Gore and will be the state that ends the political career of Hillary Clinton. Don't worry; it will not be as close as the Gore Bush battle, which had to go to the Supreme Court. Donald Trump lives here now and will carry his state.

Georgia, 16 Electoral Votes

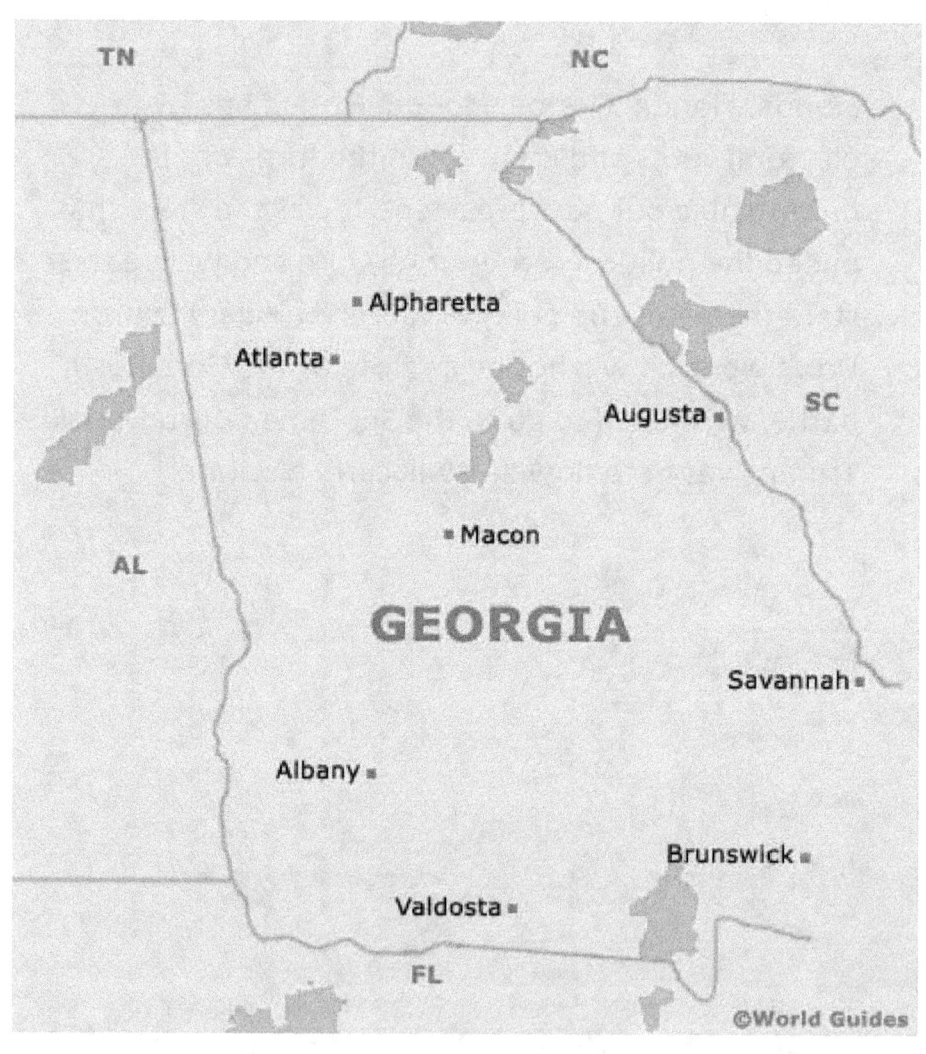

Winner: Donald Trump

Georgia. Georgia has 16 electoral votes. The last democratic presidential candidate to win here was Bill Clinton back in 1992. That should help Hillary a lot to keep it from being a blowout. Donald Trump will win the state easily, but Georgia is growing. In about 12 years a democrat may have a chance here. But there are definitely enough of white men here to make it easy for Trump.

Hawaii, 4 Electoral Votes

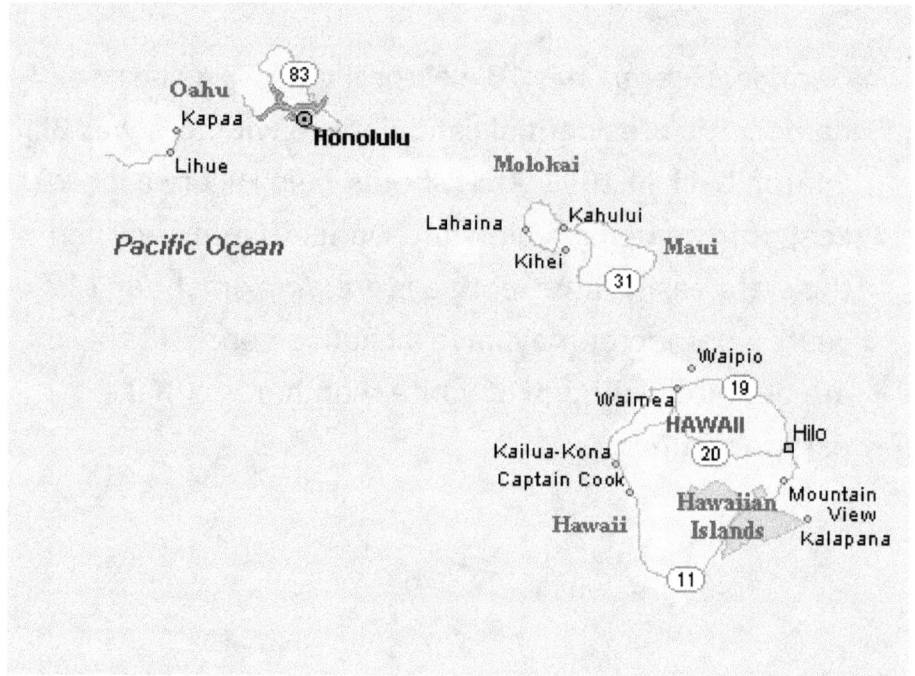

Winner: Hillary Clinton

Hawaii. In 1964 Hawaii had 4 electoral votes. In 2016 it has exactly the same. It is one of the few states where the population has not changed much. I have never gone there but my guess is because it is too expensive to live there and not enough jobs. In other place it must be a nice place to visit but no one wants to live there. Hillary is safe here. It has been over 40 years since Hawaiians have voted for a republican presidential candidate.

Idaho, 4 Electoral Votes

Winner: Donald Trump

Idaho. Idaho, known as the potato state has 4 electoral votes. Idaho always votes republican. In 1912 Idaho had 4 electoral votes. Nobody wants to move there and the people who are there now are moving out. It is full of white men so Donald Trump will have no problem here.

Illinois, 20 Electoral Votes

Winner: Hillary Clinton

Illinois. Illinois has 20 electoral votes and is the home of President Barak Obama. It has voted democrat the last 6 elections. I see no reason that it won't do the same this election.

Indiana, 11 Electoral Votes

Winner: Donald Trump

Indiana. Indiana has 11 electoral votes. It is considered a red state because it usually votes republican for everything. Barack Obama did win the state in 2008 put don't expect Hillary Clinton to come close. Donald Trump will win this state easily.

Iowa, 6 Electoral Votes

Winner: Donald Trump

Iowa has 6 electoral votes. The democratic presidential candidate has won 5 of the last 6 presidential elections. But since Hillary Clinton is a woman, Donald Trump will win this one.

Kansas, 6 Electoral Votes

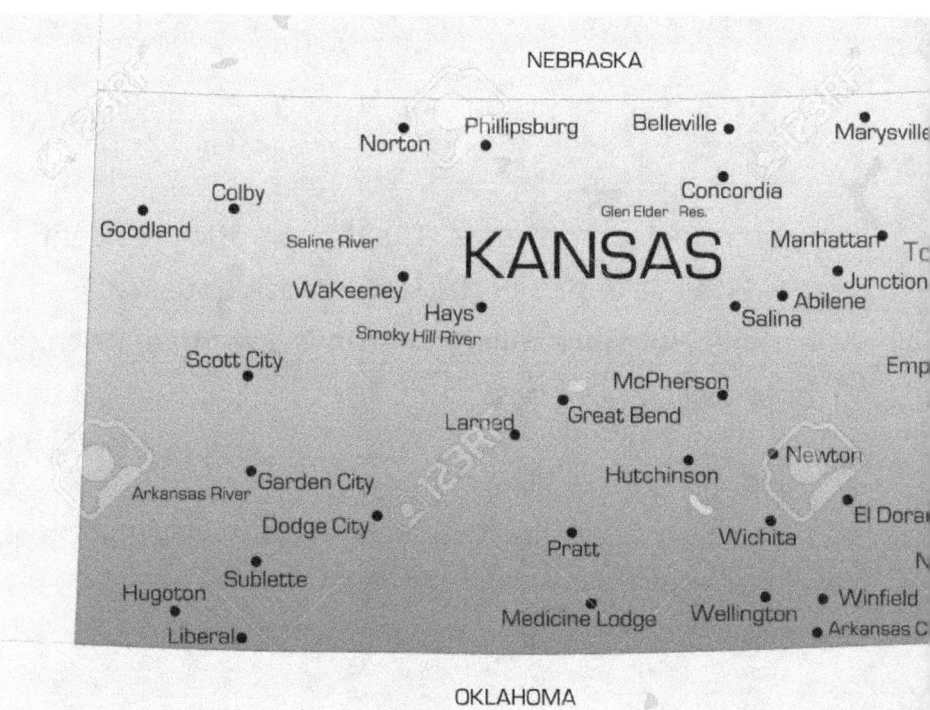

Winner: Donald Trump

Kansas. Kansas has 6 electoral votes. It has not voted for a democratic candidate for president since 1964. It will not in 2016 either. This is a safe state for Donald Trump.

Kentucky, 8 Electoral Votes

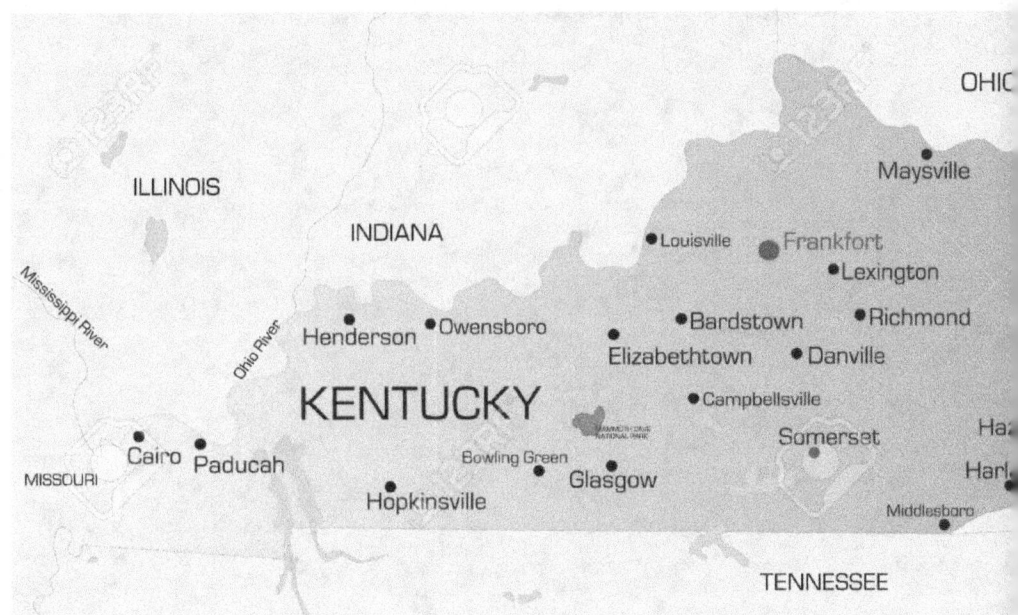

Winner: Donald Trump

Kentucky. Kentucky has 8 electoral votes. It is a southern state with many of white men. That should be enough for Donald Trump to win the state. Hillary's husband did win the state when he ran. That might be enough for her to keep it close.

Louisiana, 8 Electoral Votes

Winner: Donald Trump

Louisiana. Louisiana has 8 electoral votes. Louisiana use to have 9 electoral votes, but mainly because a lot of people who left because of hurricane Katrina, they now only have 8. Since most of the people that were forced out by the storm were black and poor, that overwhelmingly voted democrat, it will be an easier state for Donald Trump to win.

Maine, 4 Electoral Votes

Winner: Donald Trump

Maine. Maine has 4 electoral votes. It has voted for the democratic candidate the last 6 elections. Most political experts consider this a safe state for Hillary Clinton. Since I am not an expert and am going by only what I see in the future, I am giving this state to Donald Trump. It is a white state and he will bring in enough new voters to win the state.

Maryland, 10 Electoral Votes

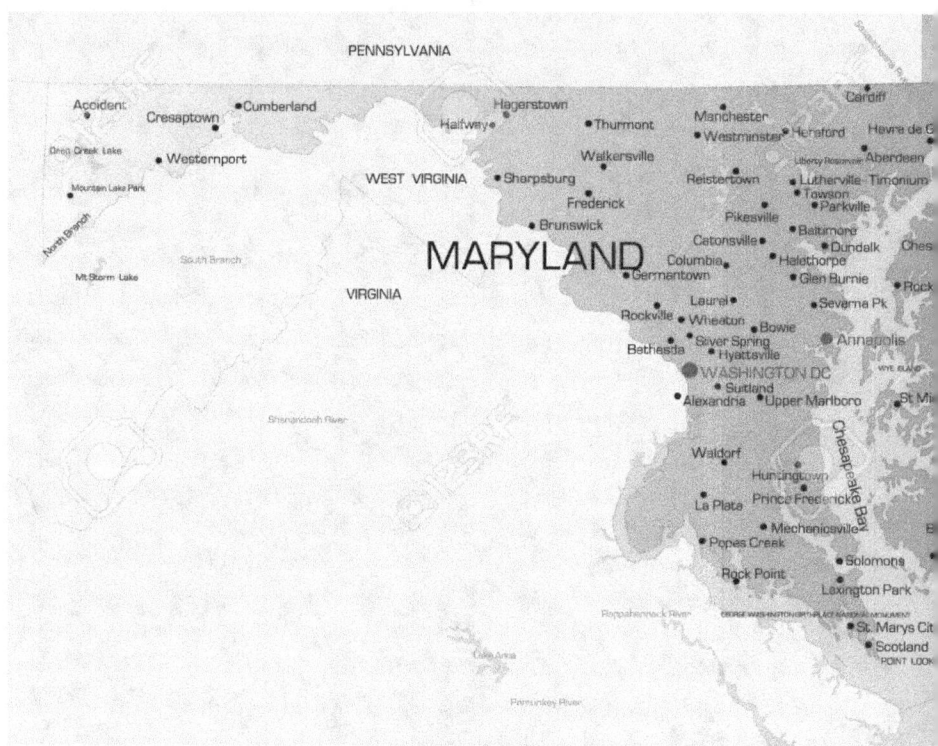

Winner: Hillary Clinton

Maryland. Maryland has 10 electoral votes. For the most part Maryland is a democratic state. It has voted for the democratic candidate the last 6 presidential elections. President Obama beat Mitch Romney 62% to 36% in 2012. Even though this will be an election landslide for Donald Trump, he will not beat Hillary Clinton here.

Massachusetts, 11 Electoral Votes

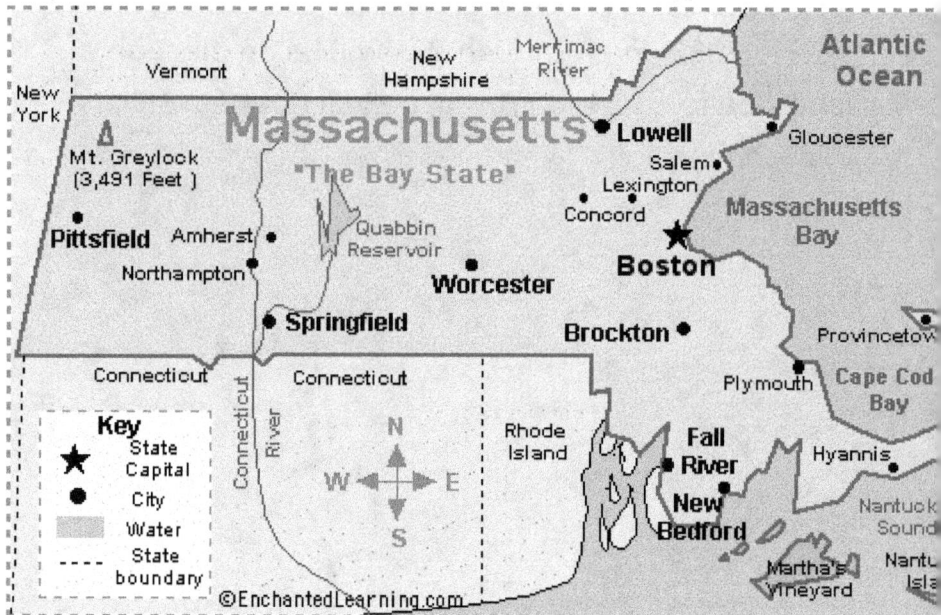

Winner: Hillary Clinton

Massachusetts. Massachusetts is my 2nd home state. I have been here the last 30 years. To me it is the most liberal state in the United States. It has voted for the democratic candidate for president the last 7 elections. Mitt Romney, who lives in the state, lost 61% to 38% in 2012. So if he can't win his own state, you can forget Donald Trump having any of a chance to win. It is a smart, intellectual state. All Donald Trump insults to women, Muslims, and Latinos will not play well here. Hillary has nothing to worry about here. Massachusetts has 11 electoral votes and she will win them all.

Michigan, 16 Electoral Votes

Winner: Hillary Clinton

Michigan. Michigan has 16 electoral votes. My intuition tells me that Donald Trump will win this state. There are a lot of disenchanted people who live in the state and are ready for a change. If I were advising him I would tell him to send as many people to Michigan. It has not voted for a presidential candidate since 1988. I think he has a chance to win the state. However I am giving the state to Hillary. I think that she will be able to hang on here. If she loses this state Donald Trump will end up close to 400 electoral votes, a really big landslide.

Minnesota, 10 Electoral Votes

Winner: Hillary Clinton

Minnesota. Minnesota has 10 electoral votes and has voted for the democratic presidential candidate the last 10 elections. Trump could make it close but I see Hillary all the way. This is a great state to watch. In the democratic primary, Hillary Clinton loss to Bernie Sanders. In the republican primary Donald Trump finished 3rd. It shows that Minnesota does not like either one of the candidates that they have to vote for.

Mississippi, 6 Electoral Votes

Winner: Donald Trump

Mississippi. Mississippi has 6 electoral votes, and do I need to say anything about this state. It is one of the poorest, least educated states in the country. Donald Trump's rhetoric plays well here. The last democrat to win its electoral votes was Jimmy Carter back in 1976. I see nothing to change that trend, Trump all the way.

Missouri, 10 Electoral Votes

Winner: Donald Trump

Missouri has 10 electoral votes. It has voted for the republican candidate for president in the last 4 elections. But some of those elections were very close. In 2008 President Obama lost the state to John McCain by just 3,900 votes out of close to 3,000,000 votes cast. I think if the democrats were running a white male they could take the state, but there is no way this state is ready to vote for a white woman. Donald Trump wins easily.

Montana, 3 Electoral Votes

Winner: Donald Trump

Montana. Montana has 3 electoral votes. That means that it is a small state. There are not many blacks, Latinos, Muslims, and other minorities. The women still believe that the husband is king of the castle. This is a perfect state for Donald Trump. He wins easily.

Nebraska, 5 Electoral Votes

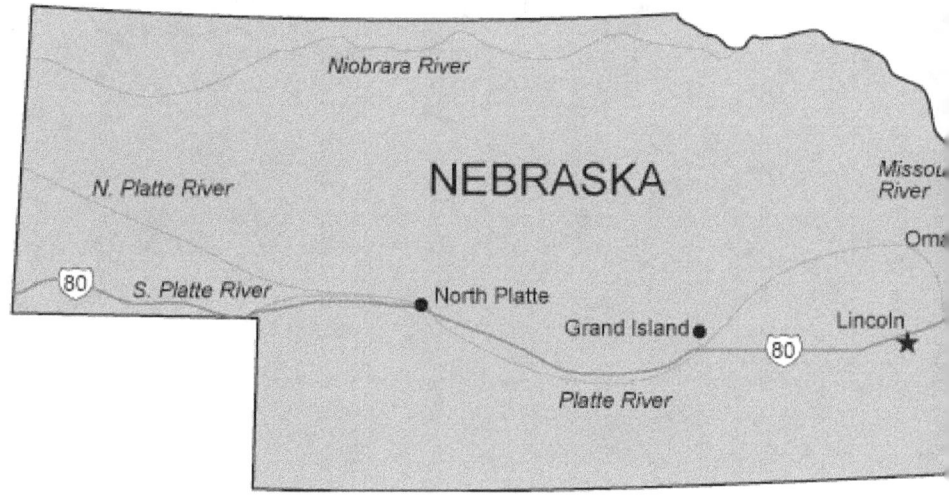

Winner: Donald Trump

Nebraska has 5 electoral votes. It has been since 1964 since it has voted for a democratic presidential candidate. It won't happen in 2016 either. Trump wins easily.

Nevada, 6 Electoral Votes

Winner: Hillary Clinton

Nevada. Nevada has 6 electoral votes. I am no expert, but when we talk of battleground states, this is a new up and coming one, if not already. The last 4 elections have been split, 2 for the democrat and 2 for the republican. I see Harry Reid just barely helping Hillary Clinton pull it out. From the outside looking in you would think that this should be an easy state for Hillary Clinton to win, especially with Donald Trump's views about building a wall and deportation of illegals. But people fail to forget that Donald Trump comes from the Casino entertainment industry. What is Las Vegas about? Da. I see Hillary winning the state, but if Donald Trump wanted to make the state competitive he could.

New Hampshire, 4 Electoral Votes

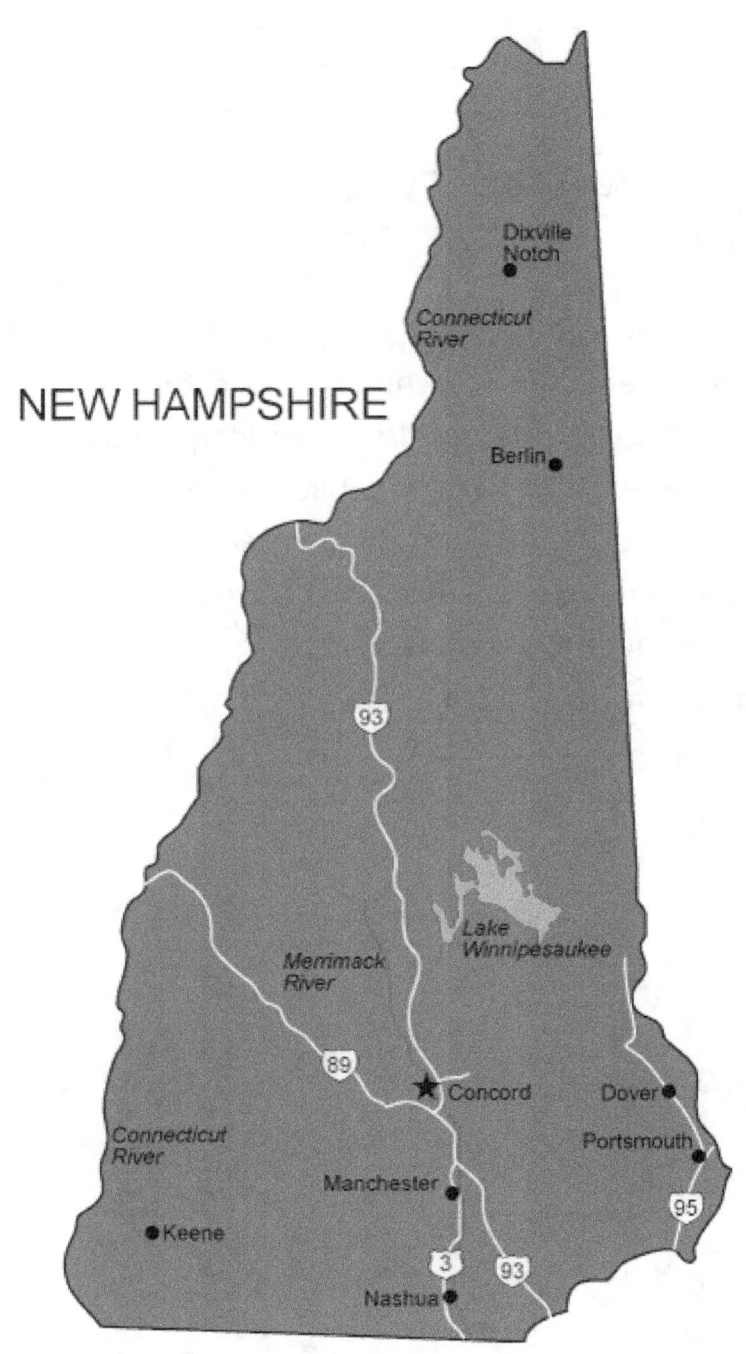

Winner: Donald Trump

New Hampshire. New Hampshire has 4 electoral votes. The reason that New Hampshire is considered a tossup state is because it is. It has 1 republican US Senator and 1 democratic US Senator. It has voted for a democratic candidate in 5 of the last 6 presidential elections. Because it is a white state with many rural areas I am giving this state to Donald Trump.

New Jersey, 14 Electoral Votes

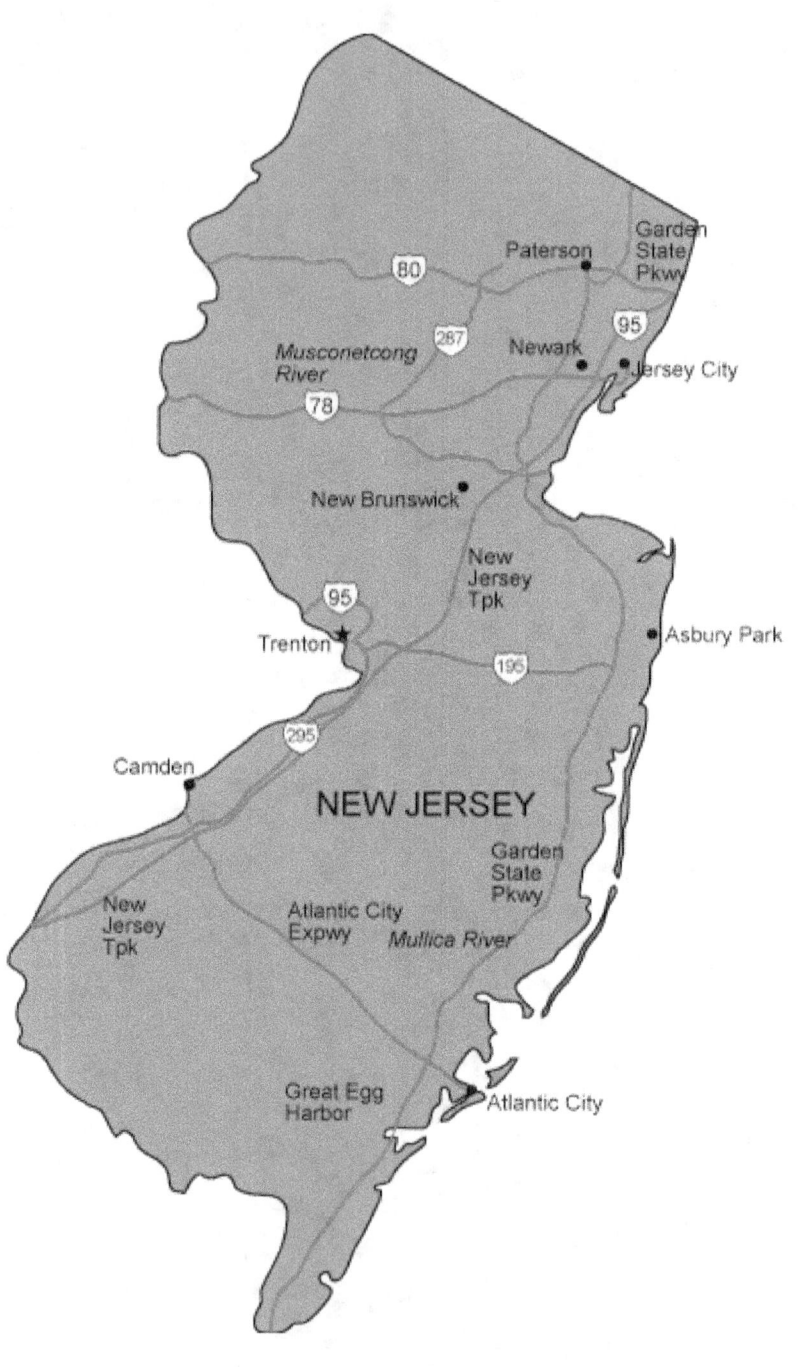

Winner: Donald Trump

New Jersey. When writing this book of course I had to spend time researching each state voting history and other things. **But one of the things that surprised me the most was that New Jersey has 14 electoral votes. 14 votes for a state so small tell me that a lot of people live in a very small area. It should be a perfect state for a democrat to win. It has voted for the democratic presidential candidate the last 6 elections. That will change in this election. Governor Chris Christie will help Trump pull out a squeaker here. Nevertheless, both campaigns should spend a lot of time and money here. Donald Trump can afford to lose but Hillary Clinton cannot.**

New Mexico, 5 Electoral Votes

Winner: Hillary Clinton

New Mexico has 5 electoral votes. It has voted for the democratic presidential candidate 5 out of the last 6 elections. I think that Donald Trump will make it close

but Hillary with the help of a growing Hispanic vote
will pull it out.

New York, 29 Electoral Votes

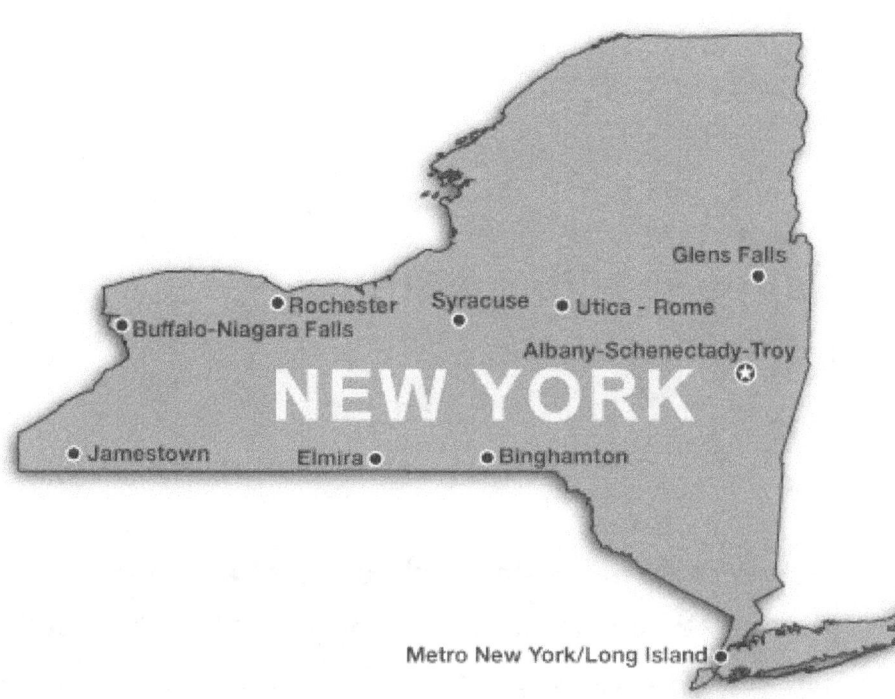

Winner: Hillary Clinton

New York has 29 electoral votes and is the home of Donald Trump and Hillary Clinton. No problem for her here.1984 was the last time a republican presidential candidate has won this state, and it won't happen this year either.

North Carolina, 15 Electoral Votes

Winner: Donald Trump

North Carolina has 15 electoral votes. President Obama was the first democratic presidential candidate to win this state since Jimmy Carter in 1976 in the 2008 election. In 2012 the state reverted back to its traditional voting history and voted for Mitt Romney over President Obama. This is a great state for me to watch to prove that a white man will win over white women. Donald Trump will win North Carolina.

North Dakota, 3 Electoral Votes

Winner: Donald Trump

North Dakota has 3 electoral votes. It has a population of about 675,000 people. That is about the same amount they had in 1920. In other words, the same people here in 1920 are the same group of people that are here now, white men. Hillary should save her time and money, don't even visit the state. Donald Trump wins easily.

Ohio, 18 Electoral Votes

Winner: Donald Trump

Ohio has 18 electoral votes. It will be the most important state for both of the

Campaigns. In 2000 and 2004 it voted for the republican presidential candidate. In 2008 and 2012 it voted for the democratic presidential candidate. During the primary Donald Trump brought in many new registered voters. He lost the state to John Kasich but still had more votes than Hillary Clinton. This state is just ready to bust out and give Donald Trump a win. There are many unhappy, dissatisfied white men just ready to vote for him. He will win a lot easily than most people think.

Oklahoma, 7 Electoral Votes

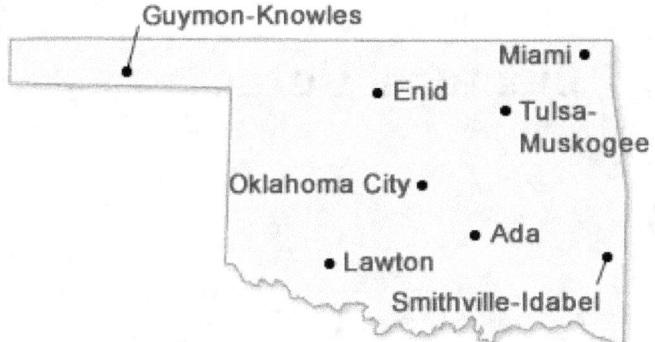

Winner: Donald Trump

Oklahoma has 7 electoral votes. The last democratic presidential candidate to win this state was Lyndon Baines Johnson way back in 1964. Hillary Clinton is no Lyndon Baines Johnson so she has no chance whatsoever. Donald wins Oklahoma easy.

Oregon, 7 Electoral Votes

Winner: Hillary Clinton

Oregon has 7 electoral votes. Hillary should win easy here. It is a solid, liberal, democratic voting state. In fact, it has voted for the democratic presidential candidate the last 7 elections. Clinton wins without a problem here.

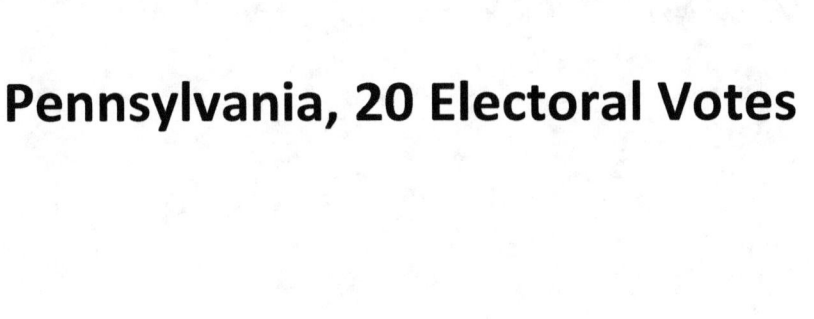

Pennsylvania, 20 Electoral Votes

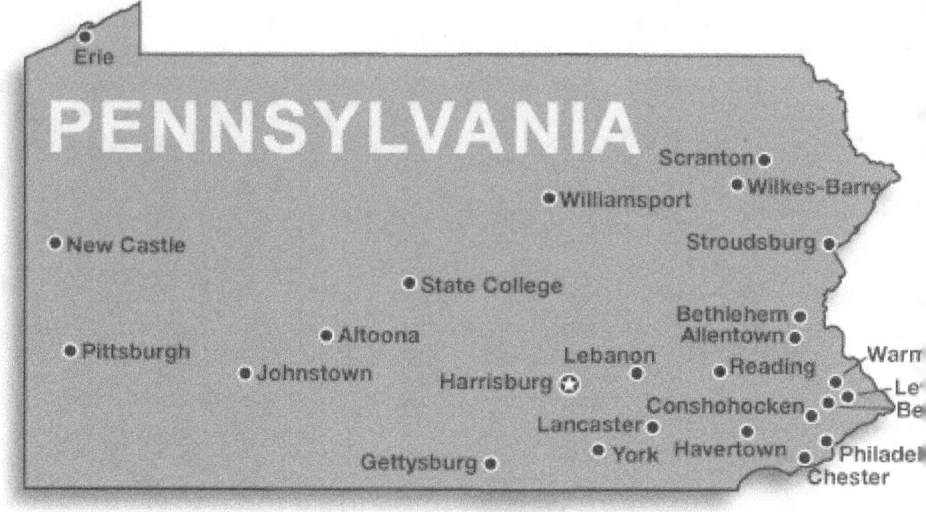

Winner: Hillary Clinton

Pennsylvania. Pennsylvania has 20 electoral votes. The last 6 presidential elections it has voted for the democratic presidential candidate. It is a state that is set up for Donald Trump to win. He will have a great

chance of winning a lot of Reagan democrats. Out of all traditional democratic states he has the best chance to win this one. But not this time. Hillary will just barely pull it out. There is no way possible for Hillary Clinton to lose this state and become president. It is a must win for her.

Rhode Island, 4 Electoral Votes

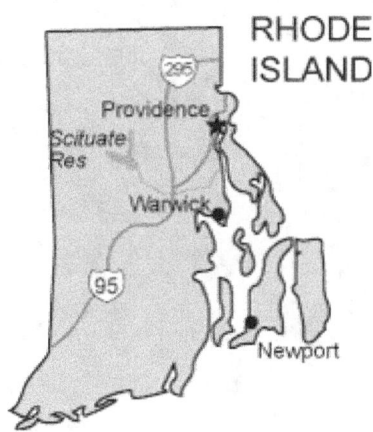

Winner: Hillary Clinton

Rhode Island. Rhode Island has 4 electoral votes. 1984 was the last time the state voted for the republican presidential candidate. Hillary wins the state easily.

South Carolina, 9 Electoral Votes

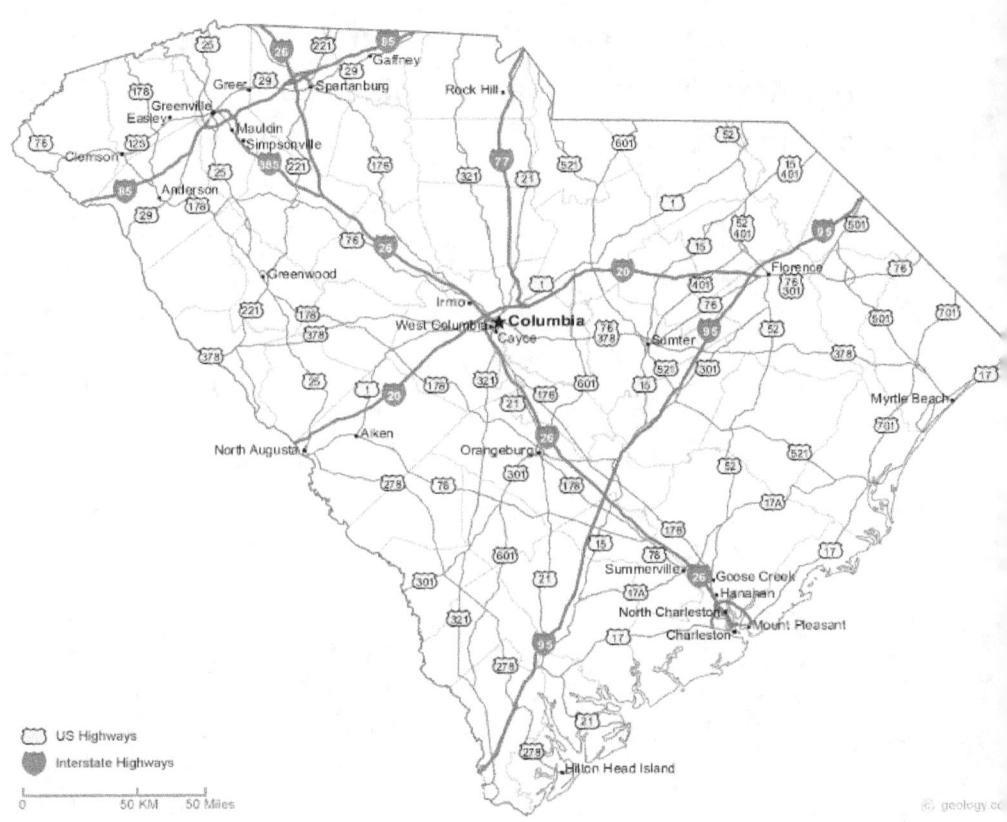

Winner: Donald Trump

South Carolina has 9 electoral votes. It is traditionally a republican voting state. Jimmy Carter back in 1976 was the last democratic presidential candidate to win the state. No democrat will win in 2016 either, Trump all the way.

South Dakota, 3 Electoral Votes

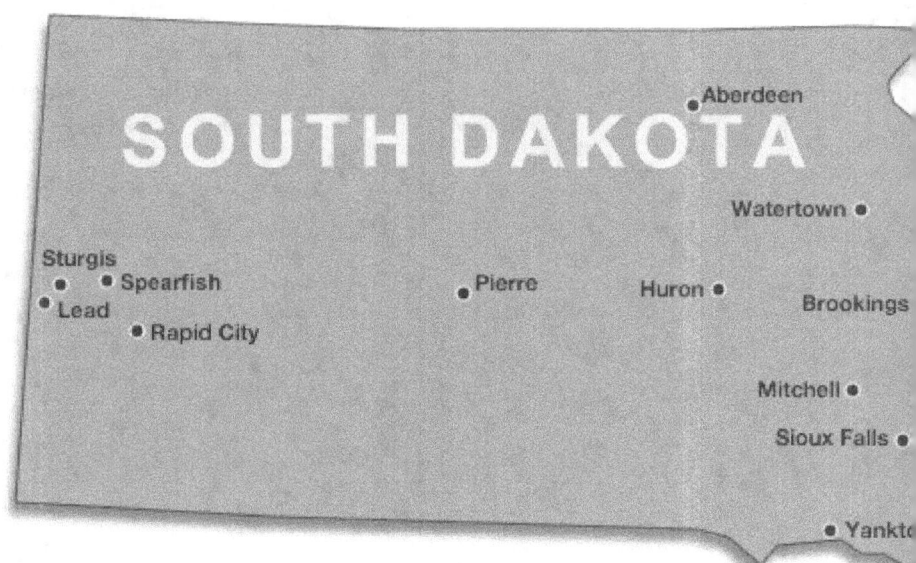

Winner: Donald Trump

South Dakota has 3 electoral votes. It does not take a rocket scientist to know who will win this state. It is not a diversified state. Most of the people are of one race, white. So you know that they will be voting for Donald Trump.

Tennessee, 11 Electoral Votes

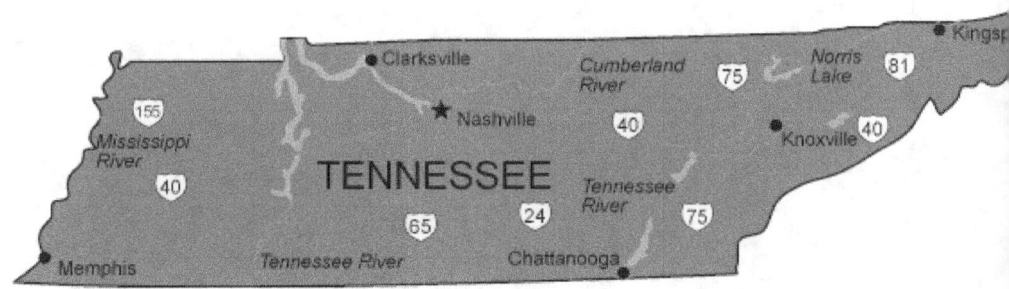

Winner: Donald Trump

Tennessee has 11 electoral votes. I looked at the primary results from earlier this year. Donald Trump in a 15 man field almost had as many votes by himself than all the democratic candidates. Bill Clinton won the state in 1992 and 1996. Al Gore, from the state loss it in the 2000 presidential primary. If Al Gore can't win his home state, Hillary Clinton has no chance, Trump all the way.

Texas, 38 Electoral Votes

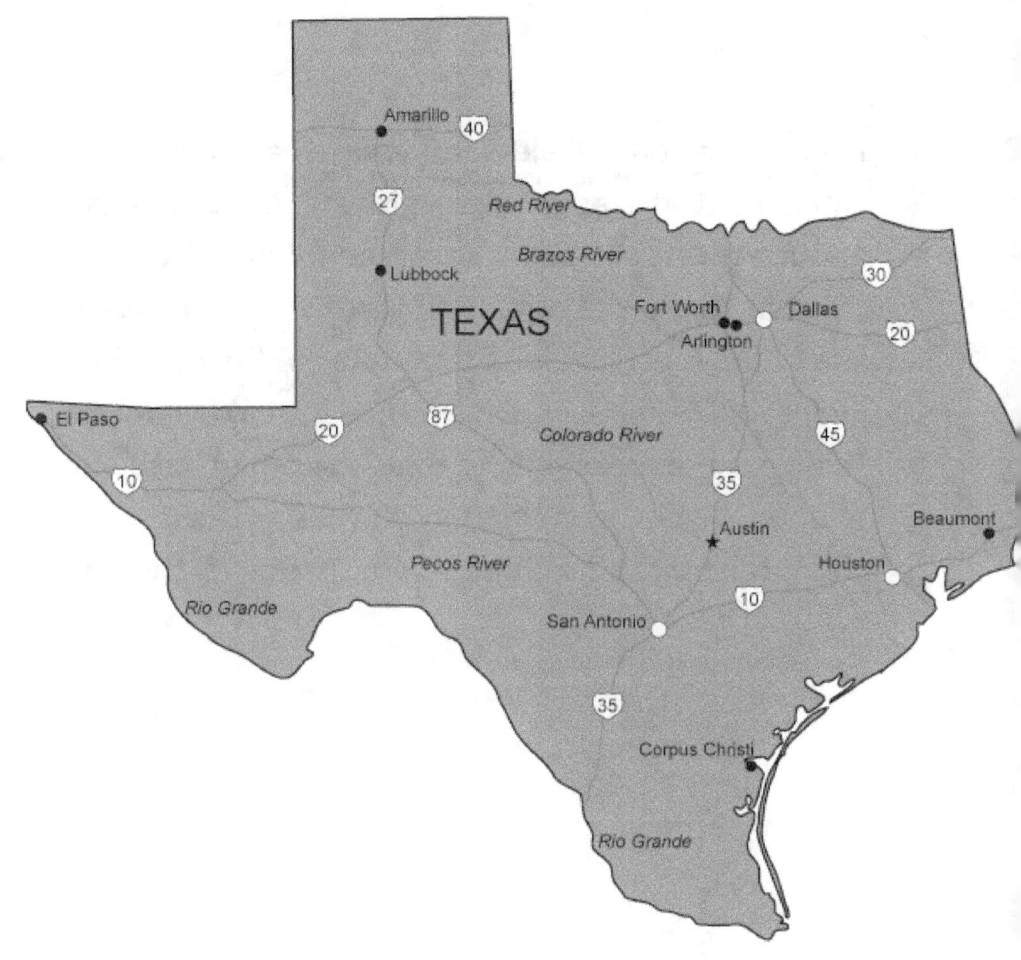

Winner: Donald Trump

Texas. Texas has 38 electoral votes. I am a little familiar with Texas politics. I grew up in Texarkana, Arkansas. There is also a Texarkana, Texas. Half of my city is in Texas, the other half in Arkansas. Texas is one of the most conservative states in the country. If they could bring back slavery they probably would. They execute more people than any other state. Women, blacks, and other minorities are kept in their place. Hillary has no chance here, Trump all the way.

Utah, 6 Electoral Votes

Winner: Donald Trump

Utah. Utah has 6 electoral votes. There are not a lot of minorities in Utah. So there is not much to say here. Donald Trump will win easily.

Vermont, 3 Electoral Votes

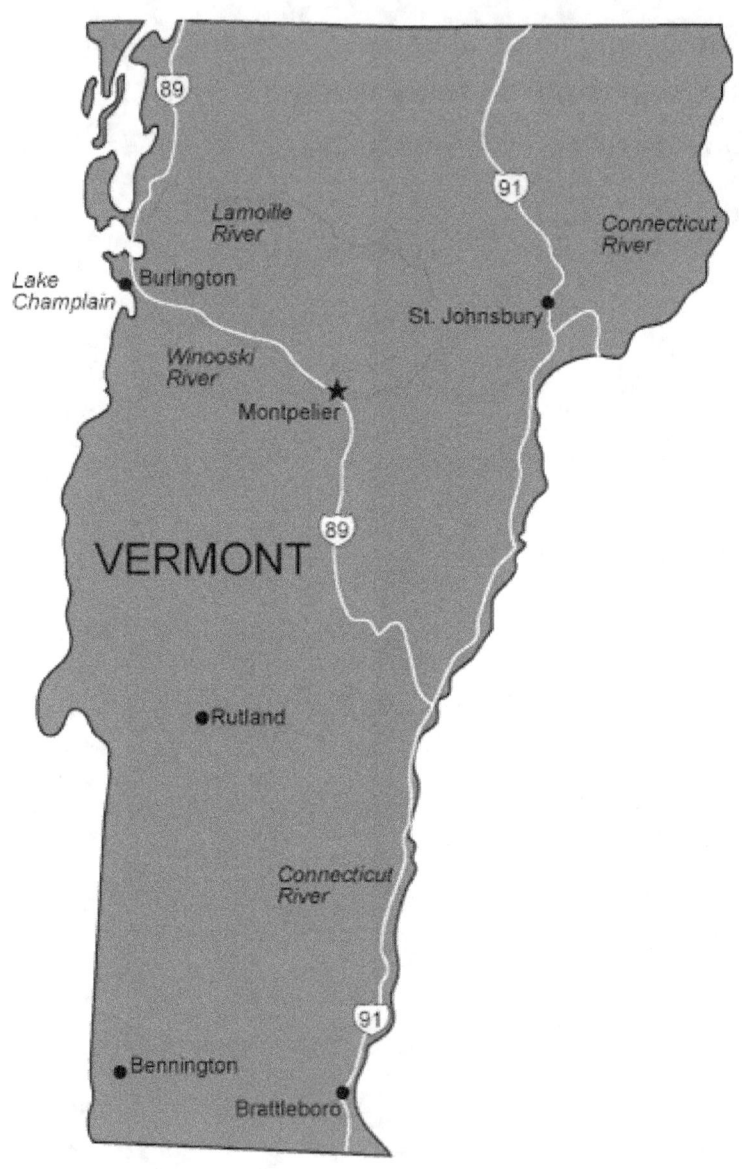

Winner: Hillary Clinton

Vermont has 3 electoral votes. It is a very liberal state and I am sure that its voters would throw up at the thought of voting for Donald Trump. Bernie Sanders, who's from Vermont, won't let that happen either. Hillary wins.

Virginia, 13 Electoral Votes

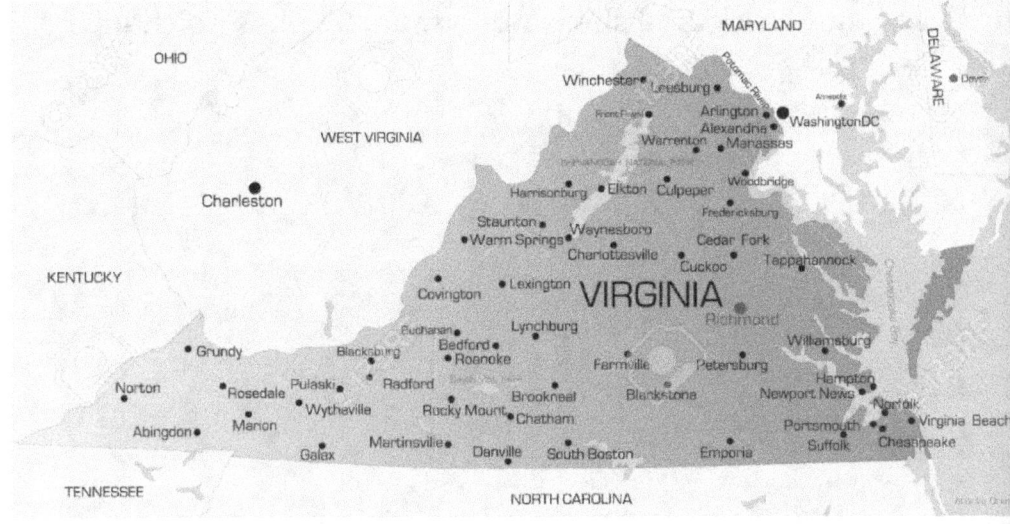

Winner: Donald Trump

Virginia. Virginia has 13 electoral votes and will be a key voting state. That will be no problem for Donald Trump. Before President Obama won the state in 2008 and 2016 the republican presidential candidate had won the previous 8 elections. Hillary Clinton is

not black, and she is not a man. She has no chance here.

Washington, 12 Electoral Votes

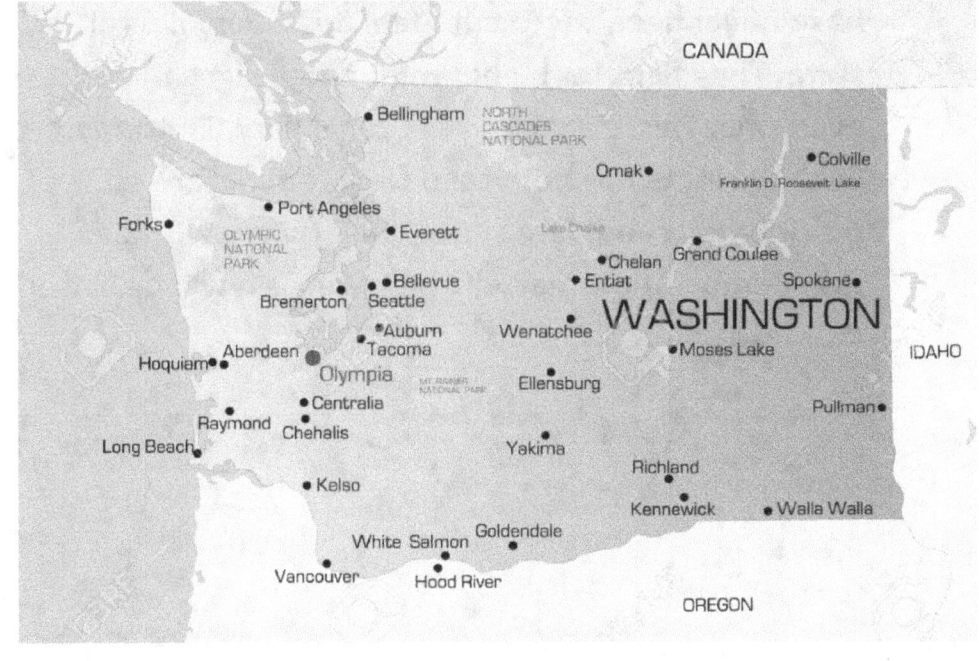

Winner: Hillary Clinton

Washington. Washington has 12 electoral votes. When I think of Washington I think of California. I have never been there but I feel it is a very liberal state. They fight for higher minimum wages for everyone. This is a great state for Hillary Clinton to win. The state has not voted for a republican presidential candidate since 1980. Hillary will keep that democratic streak alive. However it will be closer than expected.

West Virginia, 5 Electoral Votes

Winner: Hillary Clinton

West Virginia. West Virginia has 5 electoral votes. The last 4 elections it has voted for the republican

presidential candidate. Logic tells me that this should be an easy state for Donald Trump to win, but I am going against logic. Bill Clinton won the state back in 1996, and that will help his wife win in 2016, and boy does she need it.

Wisconsin, 10 Electoral Votes

Winner: Donald Trump

Wisconsin. Wisconsin has 10 electoral votes. Wisconsin has voted for the republican presidential candidate the last 7 elections. That is exactly why it will be voting for Donald Trump in 2016. They are ready for a change. This will be a crushing blow to Hillary Clinton.

Wyoming, 3 Electoral Votes

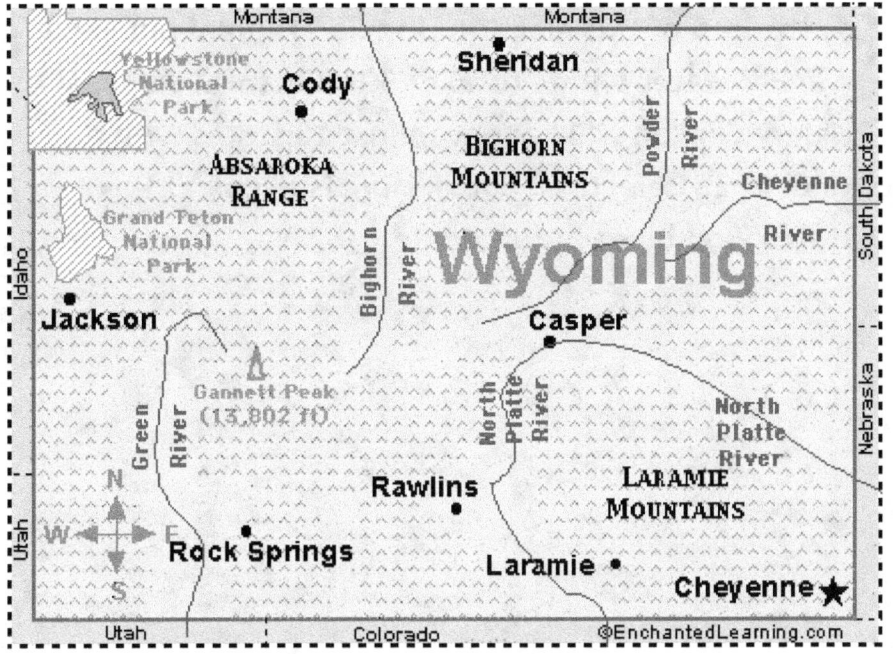

Winner: Donald Trump

Wyoming. Wyoming has 3 electoral votes. It is the least most populated state in the country. Is it a guess as to whom it will vote for? Donald Trump.

At the end of this election Donald Trump would have won 32 states with a total of 307 electoral votes. Hillary Clinton will have won just 18 states with a total of 231 electoral votes. Here is a look at the states won by each candidate.

States Won by Donald Trump

Alabama Alaska Arizona Arkansas Florida
Georgia Idaho Indiana Iowa Kansas
Kentucky Louisiana Maine Mississippi
Missouri Montana Nebraska

New Hampshire   New Jersey   New Mexico
North Carolina   North Dakota   Ohio
Oklahoma South Carolina South Dakota
Tennessee Texas Utah Virginia

Wisconsin Wyoming

States Won by Hillary Clinton

California Colorado Connecticut Delaware
Hawaii Illinois Maryland

Massachusetts Michigan Minnesota Nevada
New York Oregon Pennsylvania Rhode Island
Vermont Washington West Virginia

Donald Trump will almost double the amount of states won compared to Hillary Clinton. Even though she will lose the election, she will get more votes than Donald Trump. That is confusing to many. How can you get the most votes and still lose the election? In America it takes 270 electoral votes to become president. It does not matter how many votes you get.

In conclusion Donald Trump will be our next president because of many reasons.

1. White males are not ready to vote for a white female. As much as they pretend that they believe in equality, many feel that women should be home, not our president.

2. Many white women will not vote for Hillary either. They feel threatened by her ambition and also believe that she should be home.

3. Many voters who voted for Bernie Sanders will not vote for Hillary Clinton. They will stay home or vote for Donald Trump.

4. Donald Trump will win more black votes than experts think. Blacks have nothing against Donald Trump. Many also believe that he is right when he talks of border fortification and putting a stop to Muslim immigration. Don't be surprised to see Celebrity Apprentice Star Amarosa and former NBA Great Dennis Rodman out on the campaign trail for him.

5. Voters are ready for a change. Donald is not as part of the establishment as Hillary Clinton is. If most leaders in his own party dislike him, then he must be not a part of them. He is his own person. He spent his own money. He does not have to kowtow to what party leaders want.

6. People are sick and tired of the Clintons. Out of all reasons that Donald Trump will be our next president, this could be the number one reason. Voters are fed up with all the scandals that surround them from Whitewater, Monica

Lewinsky, Benghazi, and now emails. It is always something.

I could probably go on and on, but I hope the message is clear. Voters are ready for a change. They know that if they vote for Hillary Clinton it will be business as usual. Donald Trump will do something that no president has done recently, get congress to work together. He will be able to do that because he owes nothing to anyone but the voters who elected him.

Good luck President Trump.

About The Author

David Coleman was born in Texarkana, Arkansas. He is one of five children. His father died when he was 6 so he was raised by a single mother. He dropped out of school at age 16. But after washing dishes for a year he decided to get a GED and go to college. He attended the University of Arkansas at Fayetteville and earned a

Bachelor of Arts Degree in Political Science. During that time he also spent his junior year abroad at the London School of Economics. After that he earned a Master's Degree in Intercultural Management at the School for International Training in Brattleboro, Vermont.

In 1992 David Coleman was a field coordinator for President Clinton in New Hampshire. Later that year he also ran for United States Congress as an Independent Candidate in the 5th congressional district of Massachusetts. He loss in that election but that was not his last election. In 1994 he ran for the office again. This time he ran as a Republican candidate. He won the republican primary but loss in the general election to the democratic incumbent, a 7 term member of the United States Houses of Representatives, Marty Meehan, who's now President of The University of Massachusetts school system. In 1996 he faced off against Congressman Meehan again with the same results. That was the last time he ran for political office. Since then he has been a self-employed mortgage broker. He still has an interest in politics and has not ruled out another run for office someday.

References

www.270towin.com

Wikipedia

Politico

www.usgov.info.about.com

www.thisnation.com

www.slate.com

www.fairvote.org

www.achives.org

www.uselectionatlas.org

www.infoplease.org

www.50states.com

www.enchantedlearning.com

www.pinterest.com

www.shutterstock.com

www.freeusandworldmaps.com

www.statemaps.org

www.ingramcontent.com/pod-product-compliance
Lightning Source LLC
Chambersburg PA
CBHW071201280526
45787CB00002B/557